Royal Festival Hall
on the South Bank

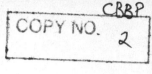

Poetry Library

Royal Festival Hall, Level 5
London SE1 8XX
Telephone: 0171-921 0943

The Dedalus Press

SECRET SOCIETIES

Robert Welch

SECRET SOCIETIES

ROBERT WELCH

Dublin 1997

DEDALUS

The Dedalus Press
24 The Heath, Cypress Downs, Dublin 6W. Ireland

© 1997 Robert Welch and The Dedalus Press

1ℓ|3|98

ISBN 1 901233 02 2 (paper) The Dedalus Press
ISBN 1 901233 03 0 (bound) The Dedalus Press

Acknowledgments:
Some of these poems have previously appeared in *Cyphers*, *Gerard Manley Hopkins Annual*, *Poetry Ireland Review*, *Toward Harmony – A Celebration of Tony O'Malley*, Volume.
Special thanks to Mrs. Lyn Doyle.
I am deeply grateful to Greg Delanty for his encouragement and generosity, and for a winter drive from Vermont to Montreal that made a difference.

Dedalus Books are represented and distributed in the U.K. and Europe by *Password*, 23 New Mount St., Manchester M4 4DE.
And in the USA and Canada by *Dufour*, PO Box 7, Chester Springs, Pennsylvania 19425-0007.

Printed in Ireland by Colour Books Ltd.

The Dedalus Press receives financial assistance from An Chomhairle Ealaíon, The Arts Council, Ireland.

for Rachel

CONTENTS

one

———————————————————————

Switch Gear

*Listening to Seán Ó Flaithearta Singing
on Radio na Gaeltachta*

The roof of the factory
was sagging corrugated iron
rusting and windblown,
sheets screeching on their bolts
in the downpours.

Most of the light sockets
were defunct, but I found
one nippled bakelite switch
that worked. Yellow haze
revealed the concrete shopfloor.

The turbines were seized up;
the rubber insulation
on the power supply had perished
to reveal the wires beneath.
The switchgears were red with rust.

Over in the corner were large red
canisters of diesel; when I lifted
back the hinged flap of one
I could see the crimson depth
and got that ancient smell.

Taking a heavy green pouring can
I plunged it in the oil,
then, tilting it, watched the viscous liquid
flow along the pistons and the driveshaft
of the central turbine.

I caught the metal stirrup of the masterswitch
and pulled: flakes of rust
fell along my oily hand
and stuck, but slowly the switch
began to move upon its axis;

then I slammed it home. Blue sparks
flared out, arcwise, as the crankshaft
strove to free itself from the rigid
inactivity of many years
in a grinding moan.

But the metal rods began to move,
their hesitation and creaky twitches
translating themselves into a slow
effectual stirring of the cogged flywheel,
itself the first of a complex series,

which suddenly became completely visible
as the entire workspace flooded
with white and brilliant light.
larger fist-sized cogs were now connecting
while overhead the huge millwheel itself began to turn.

Secret Societies

Sworn to secrecy, we were told
of the alchemists in Co. Waterford,
concentrated round Cappoquin.
Their front was a Fianna Fáil Cumann,
when really they revered Christopher Marlowe
and the School of Night. One
had in his garden a herbarium
made of dressed granite
with long windows to make you sigh.
There he grew asphodel and long flowers
throughout the winter months.
Another had a folly devoted to geometry,
where set squares and compasses
as big as men were moved about.
He was calculating the dawn, and figuring
the resolution of a new republic.
All, including the bald poet with a pentangle
under his bed, who wrote in Gaelic,
were extraordinarily gentle and knew
nothing of the savagery that awaited them.

3 Easy Lessons in Destroying a Sect

1.

Find a sincere poet and swear him to secrecy. Tell him all you know of the rituals, and be sure he'll convert it into entertainment. He'll contrive to mask this as heartbreak, but every wince of conscience is a self-inflicted act of pleasure.

2.

Ask their herbalist to grow cucumbers for the English market in Cork.

3.

Anticipate their treasurer's self-disgust by pretending that you trust him.

Grammar and Crosswords

I followed the pathways that grammar
allowed, and learned most of the irregular
verbs by heart. Then, at quiet times,
I'd use the leaden alloy of the toothpaste
tube to scratch out the vast declensions.
Soon we'd be moved on to other places
but we'd leave behind the markings
on the grimy walls, for those who followed
to decipher as best they could, and fit
to their own need and possibility.

Gradually our ears grew accustomed to these
new sounds we found we could make.
Instructors started cropping up everywhere,
and we began to find it possible
to philosophize amongst the rudiments.
We learned new words for 'sound',
'pitch', 'screwdriver', 'engine', 'being',
and they seemed to cooperate
with what we thought they'd meant
in the languages we thought we knew.

They started to be animate
with an urgency all the greater
for being entirely kept to ourselves.
Sometimes we feared that we'd allowed
the whole thing to develop too fast
– our numbers were now in the hundreds
when at first there was just a handful –
but we reassured ourselves, against
all common sense and experience,
that this time there would not be any informers.

The Sword of Light

for Joe McMinn

When the bugle sang out the last post
on Easter Monday morning there was
little more than the faintest stir
of anxious disquiet, perhaps a vague air
of something troubled, remiss.

The postmistress in her glass box
inside the larger shop would stop
and touch the plywood grille placed across
the curved aperture in the glass,
through which, on working days, she'd pass the money.

Over the way the assistant, behind
the dark wood of the counter, inhaled
the aromatic mysteries of piles
of *Woman's Weekly, Ireland's Own*,
the brightly coloured knitting patterns.

The two would exchange a look, and go
back to the tasks of counting and arranging,
not quite able to cancel from their thought
the young man standing in the back garden
of the Corporation house, bugle lifted to his lips.

Across the way, in the sweet shop,
the owner served a child with snuff
for his grandmother: an ounce
silted into the newspaper cone,
using the little zinc scoop polished with use.

In the general store near by, which sold bacon
cut from salty flitches, bread, and groceries,
there was a wall of books which formed
the basis of a lending library. A woman
turned the slicer, laying off the rashers in strips.

And, to complete the picture, in the fourth shop
on the cross, the one run by a widow
and her sister, a girl, fresh from coffee
made luxuriously on milk, lifted up
the glass cover on the tray of cakes to smell the cream.

Meanwhile the notes treble softly in the air,
and the milkman's horse stirs slightly in her harness,
a surge of urine gushes from her crup,
tail lifted slightly as the green cascade
flows down across the open space.

He is standing on the concrete path,
the leg damaged in the graveyard incident
awkwardly askew. His eyes are closed,
as he grasps the bugle's corded curve,
the back door still open behind him.

His mother fills the battered aluminium pot
from the brass tap over the ceramic sink.
She places in it two brown eggs
she'd bought from the English Market,
and lights the gas, softly blowing out the match.

The last note, sustaining itself, prolongs
an absence: the whole district has grown
sorrowful and more deliberate.
A child crosses the square, thinking of nothing,
while over the knitting patterns a sigh unfurls.

He lowers the instrument to his left side,
then raising to his temple an extended hand,
he salutes the morning air. Shaking though rigid,
he sharply brings his right arm down
then turns, and awkwardly marches in.

The Laws of England

'Law requires long study and experience before that a man can attain to the cognizance of it ... the law is the golden met-wand and measure to try the causes of the subjects, and which protects his majesty in safety and peace.'
Edward Coke, defending the laws of England against the sovereignty claimed by James 1.

Though you dally in the arbours of hatred
and wilful longing, and though your face
has already even now so early grown
languid, avid, and afraid,
I want to keep the flowers fresh in the gallery
of your hope, where, in my memory,
footfalls still echo that are not yours.

But of those yet to come. It is hard to say
all of this, especially now in days
when anger assumes a hurried air
of dedication, business, and certitude.
Try to keep your distance from soothsayers
who say nothing but their own good,
be watchful when you seem most fully understood.

Not that I wish to dissuade you from your own
best energies, but that I know the vanishings
of resolution, the free fall of dismayed
anticipation. You'll have still to combat
the sweet ardour of your mounting rage
as well as your ability to do the most forlorn
and abject thing without demur or halt.

You stand, now, in your fiery power;
all still are awed by that dimension
of your excellence. Now we turn
to you so that the given pathways men
have broken through are kept clear
of the shadowy hand, the false caress,
the excitement that is prelude to the act of shame.

A Text from the Metrical Dindshenchus

Co ngénair Cond cét chatha
ni fríth in sét sen-fhlatha
(Before Conn of the hundred fights was born, the ancient
prince's path was not discovered.)

Ways totally obscure,
fighting at every village,
dark holes by the roadside,
wild men raging,
this was what it was like
on the road to Dunseverick.

And, even on the quiet stretches
you'd never be sure who'd torment you:
a blatherer from the east,
or a slimy persuader from the south.
Sidling up, with all the promises
starting from their eyes, they'd wheedle.

This and that, oh, this and that,
considerateness the ploy, anger
the deep incentive: such as –
'It'll do that for you no problem' –
but all the while the contract negotiated
had inscribed the forms of destruction.

The details would be such
as you could not fail to fall foul of,
and so implicated in a tissue of concern,
that any departure from the strictness
of the letter, which you'd no hope of
not avoiding, was all your fault. Your fault.

All this went on in the course of
the roadside conversations. Betrayal
and lamenting ullalloos of disappointment
at every turn. This was as you pressed north,
hoping that each step you took would bring closer
the man or woman capable of the necessary wars.

Cessation

for Egan

He looked in under the stairs for it first;
the hardboard door his da had made
was holed, where one night when pissed
he'd driven his fist through it, roaring
he couldn't give a shit about anything and what use
was it anyway to fix anything when all there was
was torment and no respect for the likes of him.

There was the hole, the ripped hardboard sheared
away in a gash of brown papery thinness against
the cream the door had been painted when the da
had hung it on the hinges. He pushed it in as it dragged
against the concrete floor. And there, furled,
behind a bag of knitting wool and the hoover,
were the dark blue stripes and crimson gashes of the flag.

He took it out and got that old important smell,
a mixture of polish and paint, but also the wind
coming in high over the cliffs as you looked
away out over to Donegal. The cloth was held
by two bright ribbons, blue and green. He and the ma
had come in early from the pub, carrying bags
of chips, filling the house with the cut of vinegar.

They were both in good form, and he liked it
when they were like that, level and easy,
with no surprises, but you'd never know
when something could start, for no reason,
just the quick turn of his da's temper, or the sudden
sallies of her vicious wit that let her say
whatever she liked without the smallest touch of fear.

But not this night. This night he put his arm
around her as he swayed over the kitchen table,
the chips all thrown open on the newspaper wrapping,
picking the long and droopy ones and dusting them
from the little mound of salt he'd poured from
the soft plastic container. He loved it when
they were like this, putting away all fear and trouble.

His da had turned to him, smiling (he saw the ruck
of slack skin against the shirt collar), and said
that he was glad he had a son with a bit of go,
that he would be needed when the going got rough,
that the time might shortly come when the good
would be made out to be bad, when no
sense or reason would be left, and valour driven down.

They left him there then and went upstairs.
He knew what he had to do, and so he got out
the flag, and held it up before him in the yellow light.
He slipped it from its narrow pole, then undid
the ribbons. He pulled the flag around him, the way
he saw the Spanish women do in flims, unlocked the door,
and went into the night singing the song his father sang.

Orange

'Union or no Union seems equally disregarded in Belfast ...'
Mrs Martha McTeir to her brother William Drennan, 13-12-1798

The radical's sister is on her own
in a cold house, its great windows
looking down upon the lough. The light's
like most of the light of the past two centuries.

It is grey and free of tension, expectant;
but by now the talent for waiting
that has been a feature of this weather
has diminished. Its even tenor's now

flecked with rage. In a vase
a single lily animates the shade
of the alcove. Polished veneer reflects
the open orange trumpet, the long white tongue.

This silence is one in which she writes
to her brother in Dublin. She'd love to say
what she feels: put the head of the Prime Minister
in a steel contraption, then with her hands

she'd tear open the fissure where the fontanelle
had closed over. But she can't. Meanwhile
her writing wanders from pique to spite to crudity,
then back again. She keeps on writing 'Union'.

And then, in a fury of confusion, she declares
that when she wears the insignia
she is fated to display, she will gladly
sport it in a place she cannot name.

Sceptic

The sceptic has an eyrie
on top of the pine tree.
He looks down on the labourers below
who try to hold the plough
to a straight track; their hoes
dabble in the scree, dislodging corn,
protecting weed. Inaccuracy
is his delight. He's at peace
up there; moral dubieties
become little bees to a hive
of bitter honey he plans to give
to the girl he loves, explaining why
he has no future, hates all history.

Translation in Belfast

When I saw you again you had sloughed off
that mantle of hate, the delusive pride of utterance,
and the flab of discontented middle age.

I could not believe it, but you were so young again
your skin had regained all its lustre, now
tanned and smooth, with a sickle of blush over each cheek.

Your eyes were dark and the whites entirely clear.
You were focused and intent. Your friend,
the banker, was languid and easy in the window alcove.

When you spoke, it was of diction, how it became
pure through relaxation and the unintimidated heart.
You'd not rule out passion, only insincerity.

Meanwhile your friend, basking in the winter sunlight,
was beginning a conversation with others
back from earlier days in Trinity College and Edinburgh.

They were laughing, mildly, over the 'barbarian
wildnesses' of the early translations you'd all
begun in Belfast when the light was still and clear.

There was affectionate recollection of their reception
in Edinburgh, but all admitted things darkened
later on, and the editor stopped replying to letters.

Hope, now though, was fitfully renewing that an audience
might be found for that which you'd fitted yourself
to translate through the ardours of bureaucracy.

And these versions, now, you all agreed,
would carry their own weight, be less massed
with anger and need, and try for secrecies too.

These were to be the secrecies of calm conversation
in an alcove as the rain filtered light
that afternoon. The freshened impulse of belief,

but also its relaxation held steady
as those young men you all were once
were recalled, not in fitful anger, but in love.

two
_____

The Table from India

It was always pure magic when
they turned on the lamp in
the front room. With its narrow
little windows, facing to the street,
daylight was sparse, but
at evening the yellow glow
changed all their faces,
relaxed the lines of tension,
and calmed their breath.

A huge round table brought
from India was a pool of heavy light.
Burnished every Saturday
its dark drank in the shadows
of the passers-by; conversations
between pedestrians strengthened
then evaporated as they went past.
Solid in the lamplight its surface
was an equatorial plain of quiet.

Cleansing

There was, early on, an intimation,
a silent shadow in the sky, seen
from the bathroom window, as of
a large kindness manoeuvring in the air,
an ability to infiltrate and be at one
with the limitless dimensions of the light.

It was a form of movement, a stirring
that animated all the possibilities
inhering in that luminous weather
when the white cloud formations stood
and beneath their canopy there spread
a white exhileration that was calm.

Sought for, thereafter, and filtered through
the urgencies of hard necessity, pain,
the viciousness of casual tyranny,
it became little more than a small voice
crying out its sorrow from the tangled skeins
of knitting wool in the butterbox by the fire.

Sitting on its cushioned lid, covered
with rexine, on summer evenings it was
possible to decipher from the empty grate's
variant hum, a solemn recitation
of confused and difficult tales to do
with usurpation, darkness, and disease.

It was not conceivable, then, to allow
any credence to the thought that there could
ever be a recovery of that steady, remote,
yet intimate interfusion of vastness
and intimacy, breath with air, calm
with animation. The grate was dark and empty.

And so it remained. Years followed years.
The skin went grey with waiting. From time
to time there would be brutal and abrupt
ablutions on the blue table in the kitchen,
water cascading from the edges, as the red soap
sloshed all over pale and frightened flesh.

But the taint continued. It took a rich
and eminent crust for itself, intriguing to the touch,
which curiosity probed continuously.
It was to be many years before the wild
and effortless harpies moved in to blast from out
their plated diaphragms a scalding and ferocious gust.

There they stood, the two of them, on the sills
of the wide open windows. The day was grey
with emotion, and the brass colours of their wings
mixed with the steady flow of the gunmetal air.
Great shoulders drew back, faces were serene,
as their massive exhalations cleared the room of pain.

Tin Roofs

When the massive wooden gate
was wheeled back along its track,
you stepped into the lane with its row
of tin-roofed cottages. In the warmth,
late in summer, you could see
a woman sitting in her kitchen chair,
knitting, and a man walking towards her,
pushing his bicycle, one hand placed
dead-centre on the handlebars,
the other holding a loaf of bread
freshly wrapped in light brown tissuepaper.
Down along the lane the tin roofs
of the little houses, painted black
with tar, warmed in the summer peace.

A Wall Can Make A Difference

Outside, before language began its sharp, hectic manipulations,
the aroma of blackcurrant leaves and apples,
green grass and the array of privet and box.

In the cold arena between the pebble-dashed wall
and the back door I played handball with my shadowy self,
continuously vying with that usurper.

Beaten again and again I would carry
the familiar buzz of fear, felt as a fever of anxiety
in the stomach or a panic crawling in the groin.

Next door things were different. No-one ever tried
to master solitude in there, being content
to let the crabapple expand its canopy.

So that the whole back garden became
a place of umber gloom silently
conserving an unspoken peace.

'A Nest of Sweets Compacted Lie ...'

The shop had linen blinds
which were pulled down in sunlight
to protect from fading *Ireland's Own*,
The Dandy, and *The Beano*.
She'd make a cone of newspaper,
twirling the end into a tail
to secure it. Into this she'd
count the furrowed black ovals
of the liqorice sweets. Five
for a penny. Then she'd screw
the top so the whole thing
looked snug and perfectly compact.
When she handed over the little parcel
it was heavier than you thought.

Early Light

The wind was along Cornmarket Street
when she looked out that morning
earlier than most. Through the archway
she saw the trellised iron of the stalls
bare in the cold light.

She gave a last look at her heels
before going out the door to check
that the seams were straight
on the stockings he'd left for her
the night before on the chiffonier.

Vladivostock, Archangel, Minsk:
the long hauls, the heat of the engines,
the rank smell of steam and sweat,
the bony arms of Lascars,
the sea a place of floating ice.

Quietly now to St. Peter and Paul's
to the dark of early Mass,
the corner where she'd throw herself
to her knees in grief and longing
for the one she waited for each night.

City Centre

I wouldn't ever dream to talk to you you bitch and how you came streeling down here to me from your miserable two room affair over there in the Marsh never any better than you should be your tribe of creeping Jesuses craw thumping your way to the Blessed Sacraments at every opportunity but all this time and I know well what I'm saying all this time the heart twisted black in the lot of you with dirt and hate and always wanting to be better than the next one not worth a spit any one of you not worth the steam off my piss but to think a guttersnipe the like of you from out of your brood of rats and vermin has the cheek to run me down publicly the way you did saying all you did of me and mine would try the patience of a Job so back you totter now you pound of week-old tripes back to where you come from in your dark hole over there and get going on the stink you call your dinner for that droopy-arsed useless git you call a man that hasn't in him an ounce of strength after all you've drawn off him over the years the women of your miserable lot were always known as ones to kill a man by dereliction and total lack of pity.

Things Get Passed On

She spoke quietly to him
through the hedgerow to whisper
that she was going to believe
them when they told her once more
that the nuns that walked
the parapet of the convent
had liquid gold for blood.

Up there in that chilly light
breathing was no longer hard
to do; it was like as if
the skin absorbed the air.
Radiance was everywhere.

Most evenings, she said,
they could filter out
everything but the gold light
in which it became possible
to negotiate a cancellation
of gravity, whereby they would,
in a transaction of the air,
ascend and descend
between the parapet
and the grotto below
of Our Lady of Sorrow.

Hope

Hope is crossing the road
knowing that your friend is in,
and that he'll ask you inside
into the aroma of a different house.

It is the calm stillness of the privet
in the summer, when there's been
no wind for weeks, or rain,
and the leaves are dusty with thought.

It is the dry earth beneath your hands
shaped into embankments, fortresses,
continents, as the toy soldiers are drawn up,
and snipers strategically placed.

It is the smell of rashers frying
on Saturday night, the walk home
in the expanding dusk, the smile
of welcome you know you'll not forget.

Secrecies

Gentle is the serene exfoliation
of the loved ones in the corridors
where breathlessness and power
inhere in soft footfalls.

That is when she turns that face
so kindly in the robed
and blossoming light to look
for murmurs that may not be.

A long finger runs down a ledger
soft with attentive overwriting.
Pencil strokes are warm
and smudged with care and love.

So faint these marks they could
disappear into the paper
made lustrous by more and more
record and annotation.

In her mind a candle burns –
a glow to light the dimly seen
who long for a ferocious clarity
and who will come in here at last.

Performances

The poet of Matthew Road was the one all mothers warned about. He only *looked* like he was eleven, in reality he was old as the stone vaults beneath Christchurch, or as the secret chasm between The Grand Parade and Patrick Street, where still and stagnant from the eighteenth century the riverwater hoarded living secrets: huge toads, murdered babies, individual tears.

He was like an apparition from that phase but his territory was the countryside extending all the way from Knocknagree to Scartaglen. He never spoke of this but it was in his milk-white skin and faint eyelashes, of a tincture finer than his hair, which was a lank and heavy red, enriched with ochre and burnt orange. His performances were always restricted to an audience of one, knowing full well that excellence is only rumour, never proved. This was how he kept his standards up to his own impeccable demands. Recitals were always executed faultlessly and with the minimum of props.

Standing in the wooden porch before the cream front door with stained glass insets, he'd do his revolution: turn himself around inside his jacket without taking his arms out of his sleeves, green eyes in their ceramic whites unmoving in a blank and steady gaze.

For the recital he'd wear the tails, the white cravat, the patent shoes, the works. Then, adjusting the piano-stool he would carefully seat himself, taking care first to fling back the not-there hanging pleats. Now the relaxation, furrowing of brow, the glance out the window to the toolshed containing his dead father's hammers and vicegrips, getting fusty from lack of use. The cat would wait, in fret.

Then, calmly, the slender fingers would engage the keys, first stroking softly the prominence of the flats and sharps, eyes closed, the room reeling, the pitted scratches on the table growing faint, as would the fireplace piled with debris, the hacked chairs, the broken paintwork. All away. Then serene, and unabashed, he would play 'The Kerry Mountains', utterly chordless and tuneless, no air, no melody, just the relentlessness of the rhythm, his own inscrutable humming, his content, as mountain peaks enlarged in blue insistent colour.

Sometimes there would be no performance. I'd have to keep him at the door, he never being allowed inside, and we would laugh and howl for hours. And then he'd take from his pocket an utterly surprising thing: a bullet from his father's gun, a mushroom to make you blind, a bottle of perfume from a city on the Danube.

Turner's Cross: or Who's Afraid of Austin Clarke?

Iron gates flanked the triangulated portico
of the Church of Christ the King.
They were painted dark grey. Over
the doorways were extended the two
mass-concrete arms of the crucified Christ.
His eyes were shut. When they pulled off
the brass mould in 1935 the architect
stared with avid eyes, conscience aghast.

We would pass between the trim privet and the church
to sing in the choir; or to visit the curate
in his warm front room, where he talked
Augustine, the Vatican, a life of thought.
I'd close my eyes going home to inhale
the concept of privet, its white.
It was possible to think of nothing, to be actual
and not categorize tenderness or fear.

We left the priest in his study, intent on history
and the meaning of providence, to go
along the night, visiting first the cake-shop
with the chocolate slices, then the bridge
over the disused railway line. There we'd
offer the different sailings of unthinking prayer
to the willowherb and plantains down below
as we bit into dark chocolate, golden syrup.

three

For Thomas Henry Gerard Murphy

I

The three of us, standing and talking
on the bridge at the top of Capwell Road.
Privet was flowering, it was late August,
and the night aromatic with smells
coming up from the wild vegetation
that had thickened over the abandoned
railway track: honeysuckle, dog daisy,
and the sad memorials of old man's beard.

II

You knew that sadness was an affectation,
like writing itself. Having spent a year
of anxiety and excitement down in Adrigole
you told me one night, over pints in Bantry,
that the trick was learning not to want
anything, and most of all not wishing
to have the achievement of writing.
Zen was your natural inclination.
No applause. The sound of one hand
moving in the air. A nothing.
No concussive concelebration.
Just the gesture of the air, the hand,
the slight stir of movement.

III

Your handwriting was an accommodation
of neatness and scrawl. Its delicate morrice
a grave and hilarious processional

of swerves and delicate curlicues;
dots and swift passages; boxes,
alignments, transmissions of a self
all order and containment; then the abrupt
shifts and awarenesses, leaps, accomplishments.

IV

At your best off centre, you knew
the byways of Cork: in your father's
NSU Prinz you and I would head off
for Cobh or Mallow or Carrigadrohid.
Finding our way into tradition
as we had taught ourselves to
from Jack Kerouac and Daniel Corkery,
we thought learning could only be acquired
by physical experience, by the nerves.
'Light', I said, 'I greet thee
with wounded nerves'; a salutation
from Jonson we savoured on the back roads.
We had read, in Kerouac, that,
given the right quality of awareness
you could run down a mountain,
eyes shut, and never lose your footing.
'You can't fall off a mountain',
Japhy Ryder yelled, as he bowled down
the steep ravine, brown legs thudding
through the rocks and scree.

You can.

But that was how you ventured with tradition.
You threw yourself down into its sudden

and terrifying surprises, its free fall,
its strange elation that wasn't you.

V

You never, or hardly ever, spoke beyond
exactly what you knew. This gave you
a difficult silence in your youth,
that puzzled and angered parents.
You were the opposite of polite;
insolent, insouciant, reserved, quiet.
You'd come to the door at night
and I'd hear your churlish growl
'is he in'. And my father's furious reply.
I, stewing over algebra or Irish,
anxious to beat all comers in exams,
loved to hear that curt inquiry.
Wary of embarrassed courtesy you'd not come in.
Then I'd shake off the sloth of work and go
into the city night, to drink stout
and talk of jazz and Gaelic poetry,
Willis Conovar on the Voice of America,
or the outrageous first hits of Elvis.

VI

Reminiscence, reminiscence.
I remember, I remember.
All crap. The weak indulgence
of the mind that memorializes
the moment even as it happens.
The long face of regret, horsey-eyed.

pleading, that you hated.
Brisk and energetic, too, you were,
for all your studied deliberation.
Which was what affianced you to things:
the taste of hard cheddar from Donovan's
in Prince's street; the tang of pickled onion
(grown and bottled by your father)
with Christmas pudding late at night
after pints of Guinness in the town;
bacon and cabbage at twelve o'clock
up in your house on Mangerton,
a dark and joyous feast.

VII
After

Before us, on the grass, two Japanese girls
laugh and talk, sharing a packet of crisps.

We are inside the giant plate glass
windows, looking out. We are relaxed.

Soon you will return to your office
and your writing assignments.

I will go back to the studio, to think
again about the first slash of blue.

But, just now, we are looking
at the two Japanese girls, laughing.

A CRETAN SUITE

IN MEMORY OF
MICHELE SPINA

1

The Metaphysical Wit of Michele Spina

The stark blue was what you went for
those iron days in Leeds. You'd
open this up in your strange method that entranced.
Beginning with Homer and returning via Croce
to Tasso and your interlineal commentary written in France.

Which no one had seen you kept it so secret.
But its essentials were clear as the ice hauled down
from Monte Generoso in winter, a slab across
each donkey's back, tied to the two panniers
that swung wetly, cooling its legs.

The argument was ferocious and physical: that morality
lay amidst the appalling genealogy that inhered
in incident: a girl, beaten as a child, is given,
in disdain, the name of shame, which then confers
on all others who use her total freedom of conscience.

This was one canter you'd elaborate from a theorem
of Tasso. You loved his serene indecision, the bravery
of his submissions to authority, the difficult life
he had with prelates, the unswerving devotion
to the Christ who might liberate Jerusalem.

You stayed mobile and free with your rocklike laughter,
but explored the psychosis of entrapment.
Most authors and writers hardly interested you: all narrative
spewed out the old declarations of furtive hope,
spawning simulacra that were cruel and indifferent.

Your animation was swift and fortuitous, capable
of seizing the sad fates of those in whom self-cancellation
had wrought gentleness: a priest in a café
in 1950s Paris for whom you drafted a divinity thesis,
eliciting the monotheism of Aristotle on Thomist principles.

Or the brilliant Irish girl in 1970s Leeds.
When she explained to you how, when strip-searched,
they had put a mirror between her legs,
you declared that thereafter she could be forgiven anything
but that she should turn her fury into metaphysics.

You taught by trouble. Each proposition veered off
on its own mechanics so that you created in the head
a territory of separate, co-existent, but mutually indifferent
dynamics. Each labouring at what it was meant to do,
the whole refusing, in defiant comedy, all concordances.

The disciplines were dual: laughter and attentiveness.
Each had a slide rule of sincerity where gradations
could easily be marked. These calibrations
allowed judgements to form, and they were then subjected
to a scrutiny which was fierce and relaxed.

On each slide rule of your method there was a crux,
and when the gauge moved past this point
on both systems, then it was possible to view
the factory of your thought. A heavy tin door worked open,
its hinges grinding in the rust, and it was possible to look in.

And there, in their authentic splendour were the machines
of being guessed at by Plato, Petrarch, Bruno, and Tasso.
Their plates, of dark blue metal, heaved and sang,
as filaments, long concocted out of longing, glowed dimly;
as pistons worked their slow propulsion.

There were many of these appliances of energy,
and the factory floor, so densely crowded
with this activity, extended way back to a dark blue
limitless extent. It was with relief that I closed the door
and went home, tired, impatient, but released.

You freed your disputants from the sorceries of intellect.
When they fled to hiding-places called by
various terms of endearment, you were there before them,
the sage of Messina, promising nothing but an old tin door,
opening on the different animations of the colour blue.

2.

Stamation the Cretan, 1771

Down stairs sits the old bellman. These nights
he stays longer at his post than is necessary.
He turns the leaves of his blackened gospel,
the one we gave him when he entered as a lay brother,
and I can hear him softly saying over his favourite passages
that have to do with the Virgin's journey across bare rock
to Elizabeth, the formal greetings by the wicket, the shock of joy.

By torchlight, standing in my doorway, I can see the green steps
that lead down to his stone bower. He is seated,
head in hands, as he looks down into his book.
A gust of wind brings the scent of roses from the garden
as his intonings strengthen in the casual waft.
Piled high inside the garden wall are drifts of petals
of every shade of pink, from rose to faintly blushing white.

These drifts are now four feet deep in parts
and make a soundless pillow of aroma against the granite wall.
All the leaves the roses shed blow to this massed heap
of perfume, that agitates whenever gusts of wind
come in from off the sea. At night the scent
is heady and dark; during daytime, as the monks
come and go in prayer, it is a hint of what we strive to hold.

I walk past the chanting bellman rapt in prayer,
and enter the rose-garden by the narrow gate.
By moonlight I can see that the roses have by now
shed all their petals; the night winds are making
arabesques amongst their shifting mass against the wall.
I must think it out. I must make it hold,
the severity of a thought that's all effortless consistency.

The Virgin dominates the world of flowers.
She is every where breathing in their slight and lustrous
movements. In her the world is nothing else
than abundance of pink and elegant roses,
whether all disserved and severally disposed in petals,
or organized in a firm composure before heat and light
undo the tight formations generated in the root each year.

At the centre of her womb there burns the idea
of roses: more like a lamp to light the terrible centuries
or a lotus flower to win all hearts to ease.
But it is there, a filament burning with nerves of flesh.
She is sustained in her foetal concentration by a vast
unfolding rosebloom, that is her pink light,
wherein she cools her feet and notices what must be borne.

What must be borne is nothing less than the entire
animation of the physical world. Above her head
there is the permanent exfoliation of the galaxies,
while beneath her and all around there thrive the rabid
anxieties of the sorrowful and furious and ill.
In her keeping always the man and woman of everything,
each one now wearing, for genitals, the virgin's glowing rose.

The nightwinds fall off Crete: I climb to the turrets
and touch the cannons' silvered mouths. They are still warm.
I feel so peaceful when I touch this heavy iron
and approve the pyramids of cannonballs emplaced
along these fortifications every twenty yards or so.
The guns are dark against the turquoise sea by day,
by night they look to heaven and recall the forge's rosy heat.

3.

Sketch 1
Michele Spina & Emma Barelli

I met him first in the Jeffares' drawing room in Leeds. He and his wife
Emma were different in that gathering. I remember there was a cheer-
ful Vice-Chancellor from (I think) Sheffield who came to the fancy

dress party (for that was what it was) as 'Dr Who'. This was 1971 and England still retained some form of radical innocence. But even though Jeanne and Derry Jeffares gave parties that were legendary for their catholicity (and the generosity of the hosts) nevertheless Emma and Michele had a touch of strangeness about them even in so accommodating a company. They were animated by what I later came to know as energia. Not energy, as in, say, the kind of rabid enthusiast that seizes your attention at gatherings, who creates a perturbation of the mind and an actual agitation of the body: armpits weep, a thin trickle of sweat goes down the inside of your shirt to lodge coldly in your waistband. No, this energia was not of the beseeching kind. It had scope as well as vivacity, depth as well as a wealth of interest and animation. It was a product of the imagination, functioning in the practical sphere of society. Their limitless curiosity (and kindness) were evident in the grave consideration they gave to what were, I have no doubt, my own facile pronouncements on art and artists. Callow out of Cork, I had a sensibility that was avid enough, God knows, but it hurtled everywhere, in a variety of assertion and condescension. This they stoically endured; they 'paid attention'. This phrase, by the way, was one of Michele's commonsensical guides, which assisted him, possessed of a mind totally free of prejudice and entirely given to the most comprehensive activity of enquiry, in keeping always a steadfast course: he 'paid attention' to everything and everyone.

As I found, on numerous occasions subsequently, he and Emma were complete democrats of the intellect. Their curiosity embraced every possible mental ability and type. He was the first to accuse himself of being 'a stupid'; no-one was beyond consideration as long as whatever labour of thought or of life they had embarked upon was conducted honestly. Their disdain, and Michele's derision, was reserved for those who strutted dishonestly in whatever they were engaged upon. He was hilarious in describing the inanity of Mussolini's fascists in the 1930s; or while ridiculing the vapid solemnity of an ill-informed and ill-read professor of modern languages. Perhaps, to convey his metaphysical wit, I should try to give an example of this method of caricature. He would describe, say, a fatuous academic, who specialized in Italian literature, seeking to explain Romanticism. He would do the whole thing: frown, sigh, support his head in his hands, then come out with an oracular declaration such as: 'Italian Romanticism has within it a dark theology of extreme agony'. Or Michele would describe a poet's smile, whose theatrically sombre reluctance to be genial was notorious, as 'a gleam upon the casket of his ego'. When he'd indulge in these (always generous and kindly) comedic strokes, Michele's brows would beetle with mirth. The two large tufts of hair would escalate up and down in glee, as he would, between peals of laughter, take another drag of his beloved fag, or sip from his favoured Chianti. I do not think he (or Emma) ever arraigned anyone; they were incapable of accusation. He, certainly, was so conscious of a darkness in himself that he would never take the liberty of finding fault with the actions or thoughts of others, except in so far as they betrayed themselves into dishonesty, but here always (as with the Mussolini ferriculi – iron bottoms, so called because of their ability to outlast others on committees, thereby securing and maintaining power) his targets were generalized in the true manner of the old Roman comedy.

What upset and baffled them (even as they strove to forgive and exonerate) was above all, I think, unkindness. For them unkindness was a failure of flexibility, of imagination, of energia. It hurt them, not because of the wrong done to them (and there were such wrongs, vicious wrongs, as can only happen in the mean-heartedness of the academic community) but because the air of the world which all had to breathe had suffered a contamination. They taught the resolve of the old virtues, their reliable sturdiness: loyalty to friends was paramount; the capacity to tell the truth and the integrity always to make the attempt to express it; generosity; and chastity, not in any sense of denial, but chastity of the emotions, the unwillingness to allow access to that gladdening impulse at the misfortunes of others.

With them I always had the feeling that I was in the presence of two very good people. Sometimes, in my own pride of heart, I'd approve myself as more 'worldly-wise' than they; and I would, on occasion, be unable to resist the sly temptation of painting others in the colours of my own misanthropy. This would trouble them but Michele would always break the grim lock of my preoccupation with evil motives and destructive impulses to find a more equable vantage, one less injurious to the person or group I was attempting to darken, but also

57

less hurtful in general. Michele was a good man.

I think I have been fortunate enough in my lifetime to have met a half-dozen good people. Utterly and totally good, without admixture. Michele is one of these; as is Emma. How many truly good people have drawn breath this century? More than we imagine, perhaps, in our bunkers of guilt and recrimination.

4.

Sketch 2:
Michele: His Aspect

Michele was a handsome man. When I knew him first, he was already middle-aged, but his startling good looks were still in evidence. His hair had greyed, somewhat, but it was thick and lustrous, and of a colour difficult to describe. An even mixture of grey and white, these tones combined to give it a shade of pewter, lightened and darkened throughout its thick curling body. He was olive-skinned, darkening to a burnished bronze. The senatorial face was mobile, with active, humorous eyebrows; his eyes were open and clear. The mouth, firm but often twitching, was set in a lower face lined and creased with thought and suffering; he would joke about the number of operations he'd had – seventeen, eighteen; and when I would visit him in hospital or phone after his nineteenth or twentieth, I would always hazard a guess at the figure he'd clocked up now. But the face was a serious and commanding one: in a judge, mirthlessly composed, it would have struck terror into the heart of the defendant; but in a poet-philosopher and comedian, roles Michele effortlessly conjoined, this harsh physiognomy mitigated into gentleness and charitable tolerance. The vigour of that head, product of the breeding, manners, and dignity of centuries, gave him the opportunity of fooling with gravity itself in his own demeanour.

He dressed always slightly formally – dark- or light-grey suits, white shirts, sober socks, decorous shoes. He used cologne generously and his physique exuded animation and serenity. He was easy to be with. When he sat, he was relaxed, a point always evident in the stillness of his feet, which he scarcely ever moved while seated. But his upper body would frequently, in illustration of some obscure point, sway and gesticulate; or sometimes he would flail the air with an arm to show how a young man once peremptorily dealt with a dog in office in Sicily.

Michele Spina was a Sicilian. He came from Messina. He inhabited the Greek and Roman worlds. He knew in himself the serene fury of Plato, the terror and fear of Seneca. He was the godfather of my second son, Egan.

August 1995
Analipsi
Crete

For Caitlín Maude, Dead Fifteen Years

Look down, look down
from that height
at the small thing
at the side of the road.

A black bird turning around
with its one good wing,
driving itself into the pain
of that other, shattered one.

Funeral Elegy

for Bríd O'Riordan

The tender evidences of control are
everywhere: the worn declension
of the limestone steps from the quay
down to the soft green water;

the pink eminence of the church
shrouded in its evening haze over
the city swimming with anticipation
now that the day's work is drawing down.

And my brother, striding across the car park,
tall and slender in his long blue coat,
to extend his hand to the grieving relative
as the light tightens outside the basilica of red brick.

When the coffin-bearers carry their burden
down the steps, soft plumes of breath
mix with the assiduous exercise
of the light unfolding as they stand, now still.

There is a drift of conversation, moving
between the possibilities established and released
by each and every gathering of voices
which interchange then flow away again.

The casket, with its brassy side-grips, varnished wood,
slides along the rollers in a scent of hyacinths
and sweet chrysanthemums. The door
is closed with a warm thud by the driver.

Beneath the portico groups of people
are variously dispersed. There is the shock
of finery. The girls are carefully made up:
new shoes, sheet tights, elegant black.

The familiar bends to a new accommodation
as the limousine moves away. We talk
of the different airs and graces of a city
that prides itself on its steep elevations.

We are dropping down from the hills above
the city back to the divisions of the river.
The town offers itself to the sea; ocean-going
cargo-ships come up almost to the City Hall.

The limo's ventilators take in the faintest trace
of the river's sewage, a redolent insinuation
that is a sharp reminder of the lives
passing through these streets, alleyways, and lanes.

Beneath the striped canopy of Roche's Stores
there is the customary evening crowd who wait
for buses out to Ballyphehane, Bishopstown,
Turner's Cross, Ballinlough, Farnanes.

We are going south to the graveyard near
where the woman who has gone was once
apprentice to a dressmaker off
the Curragh Road in a tiny terraced house.

There she looked calmly into the future,
a blankness unimaginable as the sea's
ferocious life, and strove only to perfect
the hidden stitches that gave a coat its line and cut.

She would have had, by some hint
from off the light one August afternoon,
or on a morning tense with prayer
after the harvests of late September,

an indication that her way would be
toilsome and difficult, but not beyond
her power to cope with. She'd know
that happiness would ambush both her children.

That was early on. A firmer outline
grew around that vacancy she did not fear
but anticipated as her days wore on.
She was always ready from her often being alone.

We turned towards the setting sun as the words
were spoken to the brilliant air. Slowly
we walked back to the limousine, past
memorials lamenting all unwritten history.

For Brian and Denise
after the Death by Burning of their son Oisin

He was destined for the long winds
and the dark turnings of the open road
at nightfall when all had gone to rest.

When we had drawn closer to the fire
for comfort in the nights that, we were told,
were full of threat, he got ready for the road.

We talked in rumour, speculation, betraying
our courage by imagining small rafts of coincidence
that would, we hoped, carry us through the thunder
    of the rapids ahead.

Nonchalantly, without a single word, he
drew himself up, this warrior of the night,
and as he buttoned up his pathetic overcoat,

so thin against those burly winds,
he knew himself ready for the sudden surges,
the onslaught of whatever night may bring.

His silence quietened our insistent talking,
and then he was gone, his quiet tender eyes
searching for the moving shadows of our fear.

He is out there now, an afficionado of the roads,
taking soundings from the branched converse of the trees
that tell the white and furious waters which we face.

four

Haydn, Hopkins, Bird

Joseph Haydn walked in, sober
and easy. Dressed in black
he sat down to the plain deal table
to compose, but not before

he said his prayers. To
the future, to two others
away ahead on that melodydrift
he was after.

He would, in the interval
between syllables, see what he'd begun
to call the life chart: a crimson
template dotted with small black polyps,

merging and separating, flying across
the active fabric of the chart,
from end to end. There were
pools, sudden soarings, disappearances.

In there, in different locations,
were the two he prayed into,
as if they were wells of feeling forward
to the new time, all yet to come.

A solemn face, at a window in Dublin;
a Roman collar, a neat soutane.
Deferring to necessity, he was beginning to know
there was no avoidance of verbs,

so, in his utter weakness, he taxed himself
to struggle into their complete awareness,
so that each turn in the rhythm became
rash, and shattering, and holy.

The other, yet further forward,
yet more way out, is a head playing
the alto saxophone in a moon of light,
saying to himself the syllables *klacktoveedsedsteene*.

Studying Colour

(for Medbh)

Learning once more the colour of wind:
out of the harshness of the frontal assault
there is time to study the notations,
the sudden gusts and carryings, swift reverses.

But back in the academy there are laboratories
and studios called wind-chambers
connected by corridors with big mahogany doors
behind which are effort, dedication, and righteousness.

Each one carries a sign, all are marked
DANGEROUS, and this provides an excitation
for the nerves, which, in the environs
of doorways, grow querulous and strange.

Anger is all hurry and hesitation,
swift caprices are jettisoned quickly
as new possibilities enlarge upon a whim,
a hint given though not intended.

Studying the wind calls for solitary planning.
There is no understanding its woven finesse,
its surprising freshness, without ardour.
And prayer meant totally for the lost.

Mikulicz Syndrome

for Killian

(In *The Daily Telegraph*, 19/10/95, it was reported that a death
mask of Shakespeare, found in Germany, revealed he prob-
ably died of the above disease, a lymphoma of the tear glands.)

Eventualities have fire in them, so that sometimes,
to think ahead means casting runes by reading
the smoor of smoke settling as a light dust
of circumstance. This suspense taxes the eyes.

So that to stay for a while the ceaselessness
of longing to know what's just out there it's
restful to lower the soft lids and prolong
the momentary dark that freshens sight.

But this respite is fretted still by the memory
retained on the retina's nerves of all that giddy
evolution of objects that cannot not be seen,
given the craving of the eye to know.

So again awake to the trammelled action of variety:
those woods before the house, the mulberry,
the gardener standing on a cuckstool, long shears
extended to prune a dangerously thickened branch.

And closer: the page before me, the ravelled sleeve
of the suit of lights I wore in London, the window pane
through which I can make the hedgerow dance by trawling
the green line of the box along a thickened whorl.

The physician tells me I must rest; that years
of wakeful longing trying to ransack the terror
that inheres in what mostly goes unnoticed have dried
up that gentle salty moisture which laves the gelid

eyeball as it takes its moment's peace in dark.
And so I try not to trouble what I see by recording
the air awash with the conspiracies attending
each and every jostle of the wind along the path.

These activities of things have not diminished
even though the world has grown much colder now.
It is hardly a fruitless imagining to think
that the colour of the trees was different

when I saw them in the early morning, alone,
coming home to my father's house, my legs and arms
fizzing with lightness, as I passed through the last
gap, getting the smell of the fresh corn greening.

In that light everything was rinsed by air appropriate
to itself, and always afterwards my sole attention
was to act as if I could be that vacant
longing wherein each alteration of the colour green

would be known and seen. What was this if not a morality
of the exterior, where the substance of a tree,
its flying energy and tough regard, was countered
by a patience so exact it was as if all looking ceased.

Then, sideways, off, new configurations would begin,
to shock the mind and engross the sense. Sometimes
it was a tiny swirl at the far reach of sight,
which, growing more distinct, became a pair of dancers.

They were coming off some distant edge of seeing,
a place beyond which light turned and disappeared,
or stretched out to take a different form,
the mathematics of a music ultimately remote.

But, if it were possible not to lose the nerve
of staying off focus, they gradually encroached
to dominate vision. Then they were there, a terrible
and ebullient presence, their dance a revolving energy.

Eyes locked together, they held each other's elbows
in a frantic swing. The air which was the slipstream
of their revolution hurt the eyes, as if their trance
was composed of no other element but fire.

They no longer consort with me or give me trouble.
These days I am not content, but maybe glad
that such perfections do not taunt me
with their fine ecstasy and insouciant fire.

I am waiting, for what I do not know,
but perhaps it may not be entirely ill in spite
of all my misgivings, and the sombre instance
that though my grief is mounting I can no longer cry.

five

The Silence of the Calvinist Great Church

A white cruciform filled with light,
and at its centre the oak pulpit
where the famous revolutionary spoke out
and dethroned the gold flamboyance
of the Hapsburgs. There is no reference
here to anything other than itself
in this hall of silent waiting.

One by one you undo the different clothes
that constrain you: first the long silk gown
of crimson that falls to the floor
in a pool of red light; then the various
others enshrined in the usual poetic catalogues,
but not all, not quite all. In a rush
and fever of excitement you allow
my unashamed and total adoration.

In the silence of the Calvinist Great Church
at Debrecen this ardour is between us.
I will never leave my absorption
in the minute delicacies of your body
wholesome and sweet in all its parts:
I love your perfumed thigh, the softness
of your long neck, and your secrecies.

The white silence breaks as when,
in Mozart, the heave of orchestration ceases
and the coloratura soprano departs
into her ascent, a lovely whorl of invitation,
to descend once more to where she starts
the brilliant run of trills towards the final close.

For Gordon & Elma Woods

1. The Approach

My son in the rain, saying
he could rebuild the disused batteries.
Fascinated we looked into the chambers
at the placid and inviting lead plates.

The hill swirled with mist.
We were hoping for the haven
to reveal itself, but meantime
there was much to inspect in strangeness:

rusty exhausts, battered chromium bumpers,
grimed-up windscreens, a chassis
half-sunk in the muddy torrent.
There is no detritus, merely the refusal to love.

2. The Feast

The interior was a calm.
Flour dispersed on the bare wood,
a swift and dexterous kneading
as the griddle over the fire exhaled its dark heat.

Soda farls dripping with butter, hot from the plate,
soup, whiskey: a winter feast at four o'clock,
the rain increasing as the heat expands.
Outside, darkness falls.

3. The House

It is as if no real artist needs
a studio, or a study, or a lab.
All true work requires the simplest materials –
a hank of rope, a found stone,
an abandoned lintel, and quiet.

Let me make my prayers from
the seemingly impossible welter of bad faith,
betrayal, frustrated hope; just as
your love revisits with original care
all objects that you touch.

Nothing to Fear

It was cold the day you took off from work and I absconded from the library. We went down to Crosshaven and had a picnic on the beach at Grabaule. Where we ate hot soup from a flask and watched our breaths dreaming in the frosty air. The sun deepened the sea to a blue calm as we looked at the bare fuchsias, bright and thin along the cliff path. In Church Bay the hotel was closed but a plume of smoke drifted sideways and we could smell the peat as we gazed along the rocky shore to the still deep of the Mens' Pool. At the Maryland above Bull Rock we had tea and scones, sitting in the bay window. Across the water stood Roche's Point, the light-house lucid in the clear daylight, as sharply evident as the concave of the spoon that rested by your cup.

Open Road

for Margo & John Evans

Cloaked in a private warmth
you watched the air manoeuvre
with the rapt attention you had
no need to study but which
you'd learned from the doctrines
of ragwort, plantain, and the hawthorn.

The sky excited you by being
steady in its resolute brilliance
whether of gunmetal or other colours
less severe. When you left the house
to walk the road you wanted to take,
every pathway led off to other distances,
but you'd hold fast, preferring the way
the rising incline was involved with earth
and the warm invitations of the sky.

Once, there was a darkened impulse,
as if the light had been washed
with rain, obscuring where you stood.
A crossroads, then he who'd first begun
to work upon your silence before you'd even seen
his face, was there, his importance
all too evidently confirmed by the leap
your heart took out of its quiet, the run
of apprehension on the nerves inside your head,
and the sorrow that now stretched far
away along the road's extending distances.

Spain, 1955

When we first saw the *Pension* it was
late afternoon; diligence had
all but exhausted itself. We were tired
and watchful, excessively attentive
to the smallest things: a watch strap
come loose, your make-up running low.

It would have been melodramatic for
me to have counselled you to be brave,
especially as I was the one always
anxious about train-times, sun-hats,
hand-creams, the paraphernalia
of travel and the necessary guidebooks.

So I kept silence, and waited, taking
care to arrive those first afternoons
in the cool bar at five. The shade
was perfect, touches of amber and absinthe
in that recess at the back, where we'd sit
together when you'd join me, all perfume.

You would have risen from the starched linen
sheets, bathed, then, in that gesture
I loved to imagine as well as watch,
lift your arm to run the cologne
down along its sallow inner length.
Your clean savour moved towards me in the shade.

As the days went past we grew accustomed
to the silent observation of the waiter, how
he stood discreetly out of sight, yet watched
us too, all disciplined attentiveness. He never
interrupted us and knew the rigour of the
circumspection that anticipates others' speech.

It was scarcely possible to imagine this peace
holding once the others would arrive: the Englishman,
his wife, the handsome Dutch inheritor,
the Irish aristocrat and his mistress.
But one by one they came to the little town,
longing to share what they hoped we had acquired.

The first day was problematic: your speech
ran too far ahead of what you thought,
while I was growing resentful and alert
to all the variant atmospheres that now
were striving one against the other. We drove
out to picnic by the river, too bright, too casual.

I recall sitting beside you, looking at the strange
line of your upper thighs beneath the crimson slacks.
You had your hands clasped round your knees,
as you leaned your head sideways to look at me.
You smiled, and I remained taciturn, grimly
watching down the river's length.

When we came back at five to the *Pension* and sat
outside, something in each of us yielded
to all the others; and every one forgave
whatever it was that wished to hold apart.
The waiter came outside with the drinks,
and placed, as a welcome, the unlooked-for gift:

a bottle of Spanish brandy from before the war.
You poured seven measures into the small glasses,
then you asked for an eighth. Without question
the waiter went back into the amber shade
and placed the superfluous glass beside your hand.
You poured, then spilled the contents at our feet.

'To this moment', you said, and as you gave the toast,
your eyes travelled across the street to where
two children sat on the pavement, a boy and girl,
brother and sister, perhaps, and you asked us all
to be as close together as those two children were,
and never to forget this moment of the changing light.

Six Impossible Furies

I

That was when the day moved differently,
when the stride, almost indifferent,
rode out along the street. I would have wished
the town to be empty and I cycling through it
in sunshine, going to meet you, at last.

II

It might be at the turn of a street.
I can recall the old bridge, the high tenements,
the romantic impossible windows.
You would turn once more and say,
calm and resolute in sunshine,
that you thought it might not ever be.

III

Now I know what true work is,
the continuous evaluation of what
almost, but not quite ever, happened.
A specialist in this vacant baroque
I research old ticket stubs, small siltings
of earth between the heavy stonework
of the bridge and the pavement, looking
for traces, traces. Sometimes I ransack
colour for clues as to its evanescent substance,
and then I'm looking for the hint of red
in the scarf you wore that evening,
walking past me on St. Patrick's Bridge.

IV

Convinced there was an alchemistry of love
wherein pity weltered into justice,
I watched the narrow streets behind the courthouse,
looking for intimations that in one of those old high flats
there swung from deeply seasoned timbers,
a cauldron where boiled the mad elixir,
and rising from it, renewed in flesh,
our own two separate bodies, perfectly repossessed.

V

On bad days I entertained the thought
of you somewhere in the city, practising
at a piano or a harpsichord, and I,
walking past outside, my hair going grey,
as I listened for the silences.

VI

Arts cultivated in the longeurs of waiting
helped stay the agony of knowing
I could never speak to you again;
and meanwhile my only friend
was astray on the different seas
off Patagonia and Tierra del Fuego.

The Aztec Bed

In Memory of My Father

You were standing before me, holding, as if
in shame, your two scarred breasts. The incision
ran from the nipple of one right across the globe
of the other in a downward cut. You wanted me
to see the full extent of the damage, and that
the work had all been in vain in the end.

You were just pointing out the facts. There was no
air of recrimination or blame. But what came next
had the total candour of something completely shown:
there was a room, off, in semi-dark, and inside
the space was almost entirely taken up with a bed,
on it a light flock mattress of brightly-coloured stuff.

I went in. The covering, of green and blue and yellow,
was disarrayed, and I could see beneath the metal
structure of the bed. This was fashioned from steel
bars; each horizontal strut had two diagonal supports,
and these themselves were fastened to each other
by a lower joining piece. It was a maze of welding.

And then the pure delight and terror. Each
of the lower horizontal bars, those below
the upper plane on which the mattress lay,
had, midway on its length, an ochre pot or gourd,
with dark-blue markings on its sides. I could see perhaps
six of them, and I knew this was the Aztec bed of death.

You stayed standing at the door, patient and full
of pity. You knew I wasn't ready yet, but you had
let me see this room so I could understand
that when the time would come you'd be there, to
comfort after all the effort and the frantic struggle,
and to make the bed that I would come to lie in.

The Little Bird

for Tiernan

I was looking at the roof timbers
in the attic above your room.
It was a perfectly ordinary day;
no importance in the light,
nothing strange or untoward.

A good day for inspecting attics,
seeking reassurance of solidity
from the cross-trusses, joists, laths.
The air had that old dry smell,
a mixture of warmth and the hidden.

In the far corner, a stir of red.
I thought it was a piece of cloth,
shifting in a faint breeze coming in
along the eaveshoots; but no, it was
a living thing, a bird.

It came to me and I saw its crest
of crimson darker than the other red;
it wanted me to hold it so I did.
I took that frail life in my hands,
promising the air I would not let it die.

Angela

Before us spreads the sea aromatic with life;
in its opaque depths flourish creatures that drive
past, breaking surface to show a barbed spine,
or, beneath a carapace all emerald, a brief
glimpse of working legs. You wade
out from the smooth granite rock where we sit,
laughing as a porpoise wheels by, its fins
smashing through the grey sea, in its wake
a thresh of foam settling. You turn towards me,
shining. I call you back to our white vantage,
but you are beyond all fear standing in the sea.

Rachel : 29 December 1992, Portstewart

Unaware of me you danced to the fallen leaves
in the mossy garden of a Leeds suburb.
You inclined to the slight wind, then moved away.
I did not go out into the garden aromatic with damp.

Now you turn in the twilight of a bookshop,
many years later, shocked into realization
by the music pouring through the transistor,
your understanding still total and absorbed.

This quality of yours a tilting of the light,
a movement of the planes that underwrite
standing, browsing, casual attitudes, gestures –
as you leaf through the cellophaned cigarette cards.

Then, as the music deepens, a volume
of knowledge disrupts composure and everything
– bookcase, record-stacks, till – all slide together
down the incline in a marvellous fall.